Spirit Maps

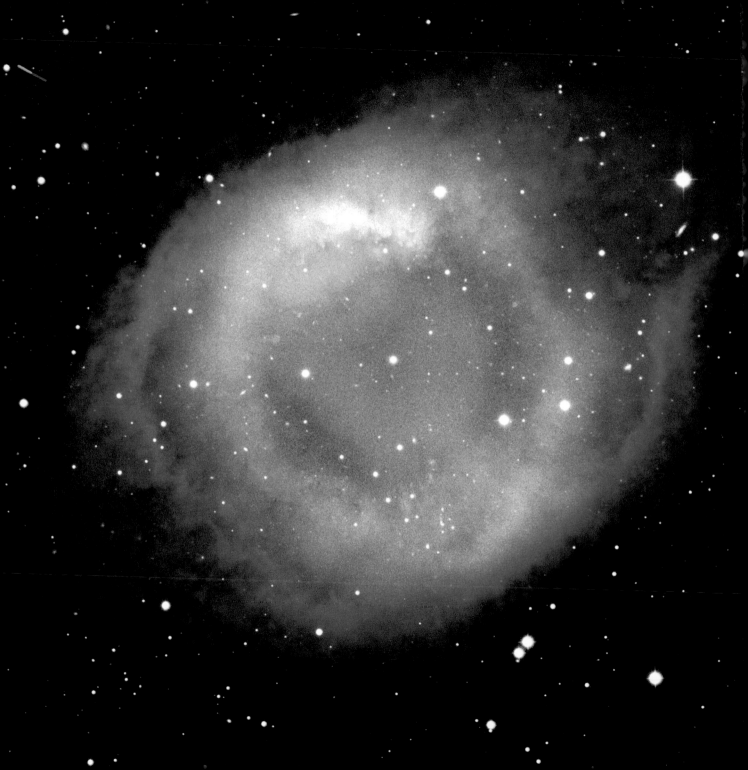

Spirit Maps

Follow the Exquisite Geometry of Art and Nature Back to Your Center

Joanna Arettam

Red Wheel
Boston / York Beach, Maine

First published in 2001 by
Red Wheel/Weiser, LLC
P. O. Box 612
York Beach, ME 03910-0612
www.redwheelweiser.com

Library of Congress Catalog-in-Publication Data
Arettam, Joanna.
    Spirit maps / Joanna Arettam.
        p.cm.
    ISBN 1-59003-001-X (pbk : alk. paper)
        1. Chakras--Miscellanea. I. Title.

BF1442.C53 A74 2001
291.3'7--dc21   2001031833

Typeset in ACaslon

Printed in Hong Kong, ROC, by C&C Offset Printing Co.

08 07 06 05 04 03 02 01
8 7 6 5 4 3 2 1

The paper used in this publication meets the minimum requirements of the American National Standard for Information Sciences-Permanence of Paper for Printed Library Materials Z39.48-1992 (R1997).

Helix Nebula NGC 7293 *(page ii)*

David Malin, 1992
Three-color photo print

Window to the soul? This gaseous nebula, "the same apparent size as the full moon," says astronomer David Malin, who captures the poetry of the universe through the giant lens of a telescope, looks like a great cosmic iris, but it is what's left after a star has exploded and burned.

Acknowledgments

The exquisite images in this book are the accomplishment of immensely talented artists and photographers. I selected these particular works as spirit maps because, in addition to the visual pleasure they bring as artworks in their own right, they touch a deeper place. Creativity, after all, is something akin to divine inspiration.

My sincere thanks go to Patsy Allen, Nancy Azara, Jim Baron, Priscilla Bianchi, Scott Camazine, Amy Cheng, Nancy Crow, Linda Daniels, Tom Dietrich, Barbara Ellmann, Adam Fuss, Cheryl Goldsleger, Gail Gregg, Harmony Hammond, David Headley, Nancy Clearwater Herman, Susanne Iles, Miriam Karp, Marjorie Kaye, Chris Kelly, Gloria Klein, Martin Kline, Benjamin Long, David Malin, Charlene Marsh, Joanne Mattera, Madeline Metz, Hank Morgan, Ellen Oppenheimer, Henry Leo Schoebel, Donna Sharrett, Camilla Smith, Richard Sudden, Lane Twitchell, Charmion von Weigand, Kay WalkingStick, Nelda Warkentin and Patrick Weisel for allowing their work to become an integral element of this book.

I'd also like to thank the directors and staff of the following galleries and photographic agencies for their gracious assistance: Cheryl Pelavin Fine Art, New York City; Rosenberg & Kaufman Fine Art, New York City; Michael Rosenfeld Gallery, New York City; Marcia Wood Gallery, Atlanta; Chiaroscuro Gallery, Santa Fe; Aperture Geographics, Gaithersburg, Maryland; The Image Finders, Cleveland; Rainbow, Santa Fe.

Contents

Snowbows

Tom Dietrich/Aperture Geographics
1997
A mandala of light: "For most rainbows, you need the sun to your back," says photographer Tom Dietrich. "This one was truly unique. As the sun was coming up, a snow shower moved across the area. The sun shining through the snow crystals created 'snowbows', one of the most marvelous and captivating sights I have ever seen."

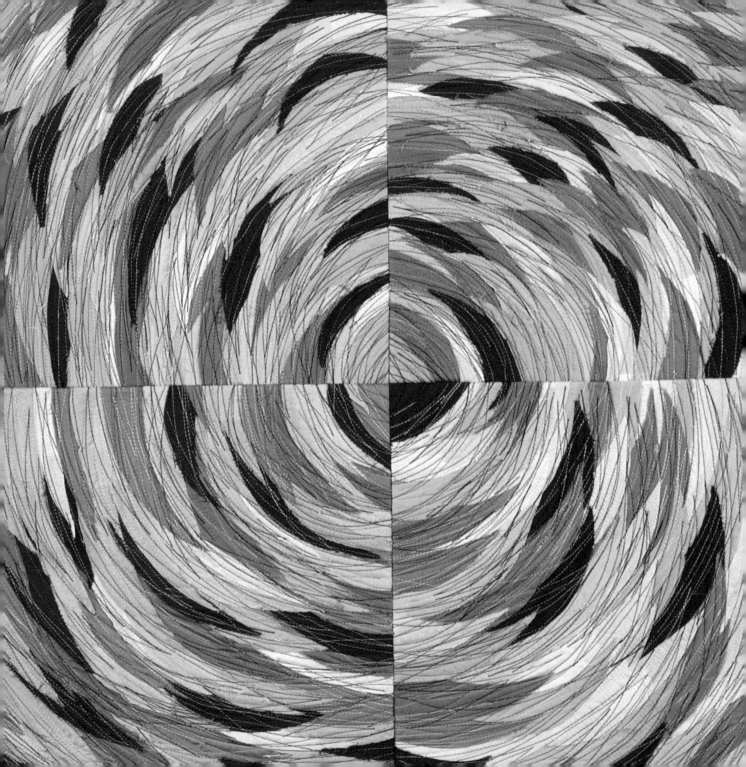

BETWEEN HEAVEN AND EARTH

From my fifth-floor studio in lower Manhattan, I can look out over Union Square Park and see three immense circular labyrinths painted on the pavement. Much of the time these meditation walkways are obscured by the frenetic activity of city life — rush-hour crowds charging to and from the nearby subway; after-school skateboarders defying gravity in spectacular leaps of skill (or faith); and, quite wonderfully, a greenmarket that settles in sunup to sundown several days a week to offer fresh-picked farm produce to urbanites more accustomed to takeout. Early Sunday morning all of this changes. Traffic is miraculously absent, and the high buildings that enclose the square turn it into something like a cloister. That's when I'll see a solitary figure or two walking the winding paths.

Vortex

Nelda Warkentin, 1995
Fabric quilt, 35" x 35"

Vertiginous symmetry: This cut-and-stitched quilt pulls you in as powerfully as a tornado. Its whorled pattern is similar to those of a sunflower or a pine cone, shown next page.

1

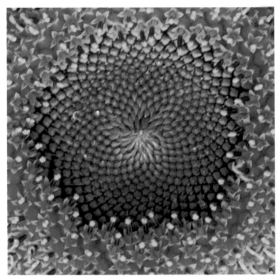

Those three great labyrinths are the inspiration for this book. Their powerful visual presence is unhindered by the nearly constant flow of activity over them, which is so reflective of how we live our lives. The path to the center is always in full view, but most of us are too engrossed in our frenzied lives to even recognize that spiritual trail, let alone to slow down and follow it. The irony is that the spiral leading inward is the perfect antidote to a life spiraling out of control. This book invites you to "walk" the path with your eyes and heart to that quiet place within yourself where loose ends come together, chattering ceases, and a profound sense of serenity softens the boundaries between you and the rest of the universe.

The Mandala, Symbol of Oneness

Mandala in Sanskrit, the mother of all languages, means *sacred circle* or *container of essence*. A mandala is a symbol for all that is. It is an abstraction of the cosmos, infinity made comprehensible to our finite minds. Spirals, crosses, stars, and wheels are examples of mandalas—centering images that were already ancient when Stonehenge (also a mandala) was erected. A mandala is a map to the very center of oneself—a spirit map.

Pine Cone

Scott Camazine, 1999

Sunflower

Camilla Smith, 1985

Nature trail: In both the pine cone and sunflower, spirals run clockwise and counterclockwise in an interlocking tango of mathematical precision.

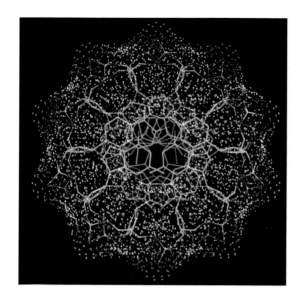

Virtually every religion has a mandala somewhere in its folds. Not all are circles, but all direct you to their visual center. Ideally, they direct you to your own spiritual center as well. Consider the Christian cross, with its center at the axis of vertical and horizontal; the Hebrew *Star of David*, whose upward and downward triangles mesh to form a six-pointed star with a hexagram heart; and the Taoist *t'ai ch'i*, whose interlocking yin-and-yang commas represent the union of opposites. The circular stained-glass window of a Gothic cathedral, such as the famous rose window in Chartres, is a mandala, its brilliance a metaphor for the illumination of the spirit; so is the cloister, with its intersecting pathways meant for walking in prayer or directed contemplation. Stand under the cupola of an Islamic mosque and look heavenward; you'll see a mandala in mosaic. Take a bird's-eye-view of a Sufi dervish, whirling in worship; you'll see a mandala in motion. (See Glossary for extended definition of the words you see here.)

Native American medicine wheels, compasses for body and soul, are constructed of stones, sticks, feathers and other objects that speak to their particular makers. They are mandalas. Tibetan *tanka* scrolls, with their concentric geometry, are mandalas for ritual meditation.

DNA Helix Seen from Above

(above, left)
Rainbow/UCSF, 1985

Hereditary pattern: Normally we see our genetic code as a laddered spiral. With a change of perspective it becomes, as this computer model shows, a lacy mandala with which to ponder the symmetry of the microscopic universe.

Snowflake

Scott Camazine, 1999

A simple contemplation of infinity: The snowflake's hexagonal shape is consistent, but its crystalline structure creates limitless variations on the theme.

The lotus blossom, a Buddhist symbol for enlightenment, is a mandala, as is the Dharma Wheel, symbol of the endless cycle of birth, death and rebirth. The ringed Celtic cross, the crossroads of the Yoruba, Dante's circles of heaven and hell—mandalas all.

The secular world is full of mandalas that have made a transition from the divine. The Roman goddess Fortuna presided over the great roulette of serendipity, otherwise known as the wheel of fortune. We know Fortuna as Lady Luck. An astrological chart is a wheel of fortune, as is the gameboard for Parcheesi, where luck and skill determine the outcome. Then there are kaleiodoscopes, where the chips quite literally fall where they may.

The physical manifestations of life are mandalas. In a joining of microcosm and macrocosm too perfect to be coincidental, there is symmetry in the swirling double helix of our DNA, the whorls of a thumbprint, and the great whirls of matter that make up a galaxy. Similarly, the path of electrons circling an atomic nucleus is not unlike the earth tracing a concentric trail around the sun. And is not time itself a mandala, as shadow tumbles endlessly into light and back into darkness on the surface of a celestial sphere?

Shell in Blue (opposite)

David Headley, 2000
Acrylic on paper, 30" x 32"

Nautilus Shell

Scott Camazine, 1999

The spiral path: The exquisite geometry of a helical shell is explored from without and within. To photographer Scott Camazine, it is "a graceful shape with a simple mathematical formulation." To painter David Headley, "the spiral conjures the cycle of birth, life, and death, and that cycle is the preoccupation of religion and art."

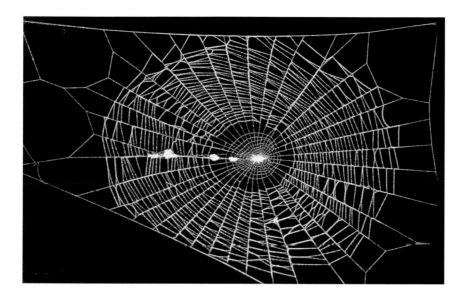

Once our consciousness is attuned to them, mandalas—physical and conceptual, sacred and secular, in art and in nature—are everywhere. Whoever you are, whatever you believe, a mandala will help you to channel and focus your attention so that you can look inward to find that tranquil center unencumbered by quotidian concerns.

One Body, Many Centers

In truth, we have many centers. Western philosophy gives us instinct, emotion, and intellect; or gut, heart, and brains. Eastern philosophy recognizes seven major centers, *chakras*, which are energy vortexes situated at specific spots along the vertical axis of the torso. A chakra is seen as a whirling disc of light. *Chakra* means *wheel* in Sanskirt, and a wheel, of course, is a mandala, so you can see how these ideas coalesce.

The chakras, which are the organizing principle for this book, unite your physical body with a more subtle mantle of energy, your aura. Each of the seven chakra centers has a particular vibration represented by a color. The order of the colors is the same as the light spectrum: red, orange, yellow, green, blue, indigo, and violet. Each chakra with its particular color relates to a specific part of the body and a related

Symbiosis V (*opposite*)

Joanne Mattera and Patrick Weisel, 1995
Wax, oil, thread, pins on Plexiglas, 12" x 12"

Spiderweb

Scott Camazine, 1999

The synchronicity of art and nature: A grid of pins imposes order on a weblike tangle of painted lines. The spider web needs no such organizing element, although the order of this one is about as eccentric as a symmetrical pattern can be.

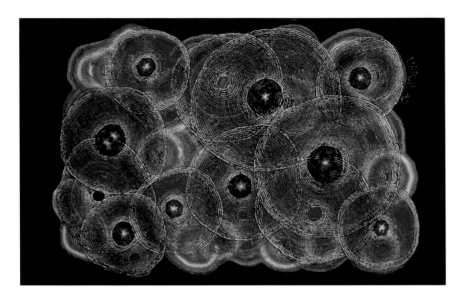

emotional pattern; from instinct, at the bottom of the spine, to spirituality, at the crown of the head. Similar to exits on a throughway, the chakras offer you a means to explore other centers along the way: passion, self-esteem, compassion, expression and perception.

The Art in this Book: Spirit Maps to Your Center

The images in this book come from the artist's imagination and the photographer's eye. While all provide a means for finding the quiet place within yourself, they are as varied as the artists who conjured them. Some artworks were constructed consciously to be meditative Hindu yantras or to express the Zen concept of "everything and nothing," or to be, as Marjorie Kaye, says, "my particular conversation with the spirit." Other images emerged intuitively as the result of the pain of surgery, the joyous birth of a child, the remembrance of a loved one or simply from overwhelming gratitude for a particular moment in time.

"Artmaking to me is a spiritual practice," says Nancy Azara, who feels that body, mind, heart and spirit are involved in the process. "When spirit takes form, the healing properties and magical qualities inherent in artmaking take shape in the work of art and speak to the viewer."

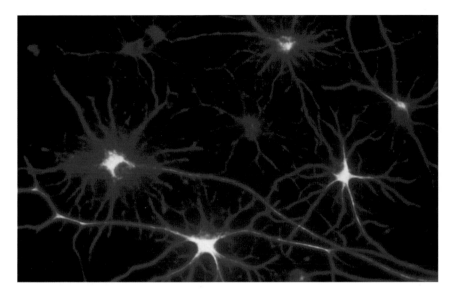

Not all of the artists identify themselves or their art as religious or spiritual, but nearly all acknowledge the connection to something greater. "I am at one with myself when I am involved in the creative process," says Nelda Warkentin, whose *Vortex* is shown at the beginning of this section. Adds Joanne Mattera, "My work is not about spirituality, but I think there is spirituality about my work because I am so focused in its making. I hope the viewer will perceive that." Art, after all, exists along a continuum of creator, object and viewer so that intent and perception are inextricably intertwined.

Following the Exquisite Geometry of these Spirit Maps

The compelling artworks in this book merit attention on their own terms. As you stop to savor each one — and that's the point here: you have to step off the treadmill — simply take in the shape, the color, the vibration, if you will. You'll find that your breathing slows and deepens, and the weight on your shoulders becomes noticeably less heavy.

At the next level, you may want to consider one particular image. Don't seek it. Let it find you. Allow your eyes to touch its contours and take in its nuances. Let your mind wander freely within the parameters

Raindrops on a Pond

(opposite)
Charlene Marsh, 1990
Handtufted wool, 57" x 81"

Brain Cells Firing

Hank Morgan/Rainbow, 1995

As within, so without: A rug of ever-widening circles and a view of fluorescing brain cells (recorded via a high-powered microscope onto 35-mm film) each contain elements in whose centers the very same pattern of color explodes in the very same way.

Untitled (Sun)

Jim Baron/The Image Finders

Sol to soul: The earliest mandala, still an inspiration to humankind, is the glowing orb that rises and sets each day.

Spiral Nebula AAT-008

(opposite)
David Malin, 1990
Three-color photo print

Cosmic symmetry: In this picture, Malin says, "We link the familiar Earth, spinning endlessly beneath the stars, to the stars themselves, and to distant galaxies of stars far beyond. This link between our planet and the stars is romantic, spiritual, provocative and uplifting. It is also real."

of the page. This is your island of calm. First, inhale slowly so that air fills the deepest part of your lungs. Then, exhale slowly and evenly so that you feel your breath move up and out of your nostrils. A gentle, steady cycle of breath in and out will help bring your mind and body into harmony. At that point, you'll realize that your mental jumble has quieted into clearer and more focused thought.

At yet the next level, you may want to remain with a group of images whose color range resonates for you. Intuitively or consciously, you'll select the hue—and thus the chakra center—that most needs your focused attention. Within each color grouping are contemplations and a meditation for that center.

Should you choose to take the whole journey, you'll start with *Instinct*, the will to survive, and work slowly upward through the chakras (taking time to visit with yourself at each center) to *Spirituality*, the desire to connect to something greater than ourselves. Leave goals behind. You don't have to become anything. This is a slow, visually rewarding path that will reveal a little bit more each time you travel it.

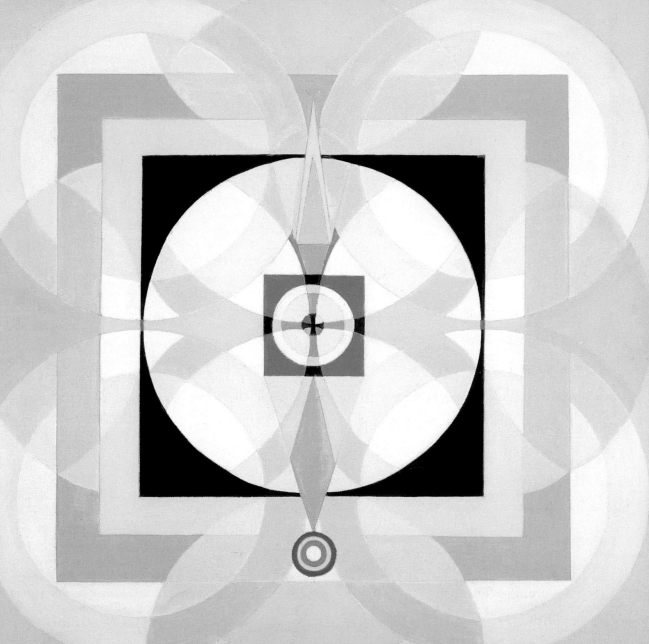

The Journey

Like a seed that begins its life underground and pushes through the soil to blossom in the sun, the chakras begin at the lowest part of the torso and move up the spine to the top of the head. The bottommost chakra connects deeply to the earth, while the topmost chakra receives the divine light of a higher spirit. We follow the path of the chakras, as centuries of seekers have done before us, because these mandalas of energy let us reach into ourselves at every level—physical, emotional and spiritual—and center ourselves at each one. No one chakra is more important than another, just as no one part of a plant is more important than another. Sure, the flower may be more beautiful, but there is no blossom without root, stalk, and leaves.

The Kundalini Lotus

Charmion von Weigand
(1896-1983), 1968
Oil on canvas, 35" x 35"

This abstraction of a traditional Tibetan mandala, represents the life energy of the body, the kundalini. "Von Weigand's mature works reflect her core beliefs: the universe is a single living substance; life is the expression of opposites; the goal of living is to achieve oneness; and reality is reached through stages toward higher states of consciousness," writes Dr. Jennifer Newton Hersh in her essay, "From the Surreal to the Sublime." (In the catalog Charmion von Weigand: Spirituality in Abstraction, the Michael Rosenfeld Gallery, 2000.)

The Chakras

There are seven major chakras in the body, each focusing the energy of the universe in specific ways.

Root Chakra
Instinct, survival

Lower Abdomen Chakra
Passion, creativity

Solar Plexus Chakra
Self-esteem, will

Heart Chakra
Compassion, gratitude

Throat Chakra
Expression, communication

Third Eye Chakra
Perception, sixth sense

Crown Chakra
Spirituality, infinity

Most of us cannot see the chakras, but the healers and spiritual adepts to whom they are visible describe them as whirling, colored discs—about the diameter of a circle made by your thumb and forefinger—that open and close like flowers. The chakras open when you are receptive and close when you're not. They don't exist in your physical body but connect to it from within the more refined mantle of energy that envelopes you. (Isn't it nice to know you exist beyond your skin?) You need not be Hindu or Buddhist to follow the path of the chakras, in the same way that you need not be a world traveler to take a trip. Just be open to taking this journey. Our deepest joys, fears and dreams are contained in the chakras, and stopping at each chakra center helps us to understand and center ourselves.

Many of the artists whose work is shown in the upcoming chapters feel a profound connection to the spirit, as their comments reveal. Yet artmaking, while intimately connecting spirit and artist, is also about making conscious aesthetic and intellectual choices about subject matter, color and composition. So, too, is critical art viewing. But here, for the purpose of centering ourselves, we shall let intellect take a back seat to intuition as we are carried by the current of color, image, and our own directed thoughts.

I NSTINCT

**Mythic America
or How the West Was One**

Lane Twitchell, 1998
Cut paper, acrylic, pigment,
newspaper, Plexiglas, 48" x 48"

Root chakra energy concerns itself with land, tribe, and physical labor. In this mandala, the artist draws on just those elements, citing the history of the American West, his Mormon ancestry and what he calls the "purifying nature" of hard work. "If there is a personally specific spiritual theme in my work, it is about the value of labor," says Twitchell. "These are difficult paintings to make. They require hours of extended labor. My studio becomes a meditative space where everything is blocked out except the work at hand."

Red is the color of life. It is the color of the blood that flows through the umbilical cord, connecting a mother to her developing child. The hemoglobin in blood is colored by iron, the metal that exists in molten form at the center of our planet. We are thus joined to Mother Earth in essentially the same way as an unborn child is to its mother, albeit without the cord. Is it any wonder that red is the color of our most elemental center, the Root Chakra?

The Root Chakra

This chakra connects from your astral body to the the base of your spine. It is the essence of physical being: instinct and survival.

Physically it is the chakra of health and vitality (to be "in the pink" is the expression of overall good health). Its energy is centered

16

The Hunter

Nancy Azara, 1991
Carved and painted wood with
gold leaf, 31" x 45" x 13"

Survival, the essence of the Root Chakra, is expressed in the concept of providing for oneself while living in harmony with the earth.

The Greek/Roman goddess Artemis/Diana is an archetype. Often depicted as a young hunter carrying a bow and arrow, she is also viewed as the protector of wild animals and guardian of streams and springs. This artwork, however, reflects a different kind of hunt. "The Hunter," says its creator, "is about searching for spirit, piercing the outer shell to uncover the inner. It says 'fly into me, follow the journey around and around until you find the source and stay with me there in the unknown.'"

in the blood and lower limbs. This is the center that grounds you—literally. Cultivate a garden. Go for a walk. Stand tall.

Emotionally it houses the tribal mind, those instinctive ancestral and familial ties expressed by the adage, "Blood is thicker than water." It is the chakra of parent-and-child relationships (healthy or dysfunctional) that extend through generations. From this center we instinctively seek to create a safe place for ourselves in the world. This is also the center of primal fears, where the unknown may make us turn away from people and ideas that are "different," where the worry of not having enough may drive us to hoard money, food or emotions.

Spiritually the Root Chakra impels us to be part of something larger, to "put down roots" with family, community, and the earth itself.

Vibrations

Elementary physics tells us that energy exists in many forms, including light, sound and matter. As you center your thoughts at the first chakra, you may want to draw on these complementary vibrations.

Light: Red has a frequency that is lower than other colors in the spectrum, so the vibration for the Root Chakra is deep and slow.

18

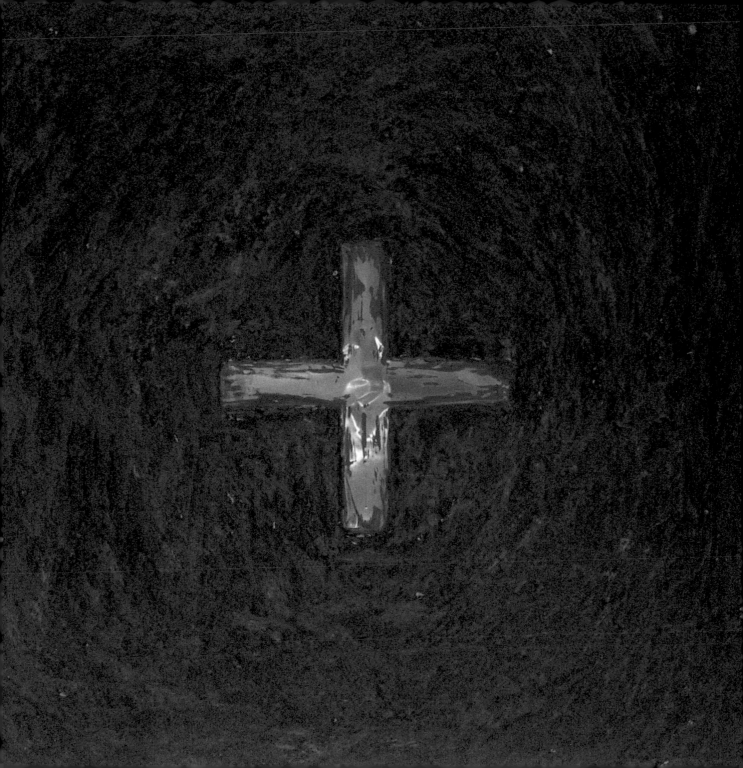

Grounding is the means by which we center ourselves on the earth. We need to plant our feet on the ground and stand tall, so that we can draw earth energy through our legs as a plant draws water through its stalk. "I made this quilt at a time when I was overwhelmed with pain from my right knee. I did not consciously start out to make a quilt about my attempt to endure pain. It just happened," says the artist. "However, I want my finished work to stand on its own without any descriptions of what I intended it to be or represent."

(previous spread)
The Four Directions: Spirit Center

Kay WalkingStick, 1995
Oil, acrylic, wax on canvas
28" x 56"

Respecting the earth is a spiritual expression of the Root Chakra. This painting includes the symbol for the cardinal points. "The four directions are honored by most, perhaps all, Native Americans. The earth is sacred. Our ceremonials are diverse, but there is a shared world view that venerates the earth," says WalkingStick. The symbol is also a Christian cross, she notes. "I am a Christian who honors the Native world view. I want to 'walk the Beauty Path,' as the Navajos say. I want to walk with God."

Sound: The vibration that resonates for this chakra is LAM (with the *a* as in *ah*) in the tone of C. If you don't know the tone scale, try U (as in *too*) in whatever key is comfortable for your voice. Take a full-lung breath. As you exhale, make the sound, finishing with *mmmm*.

Matter: Holding beads or a stone of complementary material may help you to center your thoughts. Try hematite, the shiny gray/black stone that is mostly iron ore, or any deep blood-colored stone.

Contemplations

The mandalas in this chapter offer you a visual means for centering your thoughts on the most elemental aspects of being.

I can take care of myself. Heroic figures such as Diana the Hunter and Athena the Warrior embody the archetype of self-sufficiency. You may no longer know how to start a fire or spear a fish, but you go off to work each day to pay the electric bill and buy groceries — and often, not only for yourself, but for others. As you make your place in the world, consider these related ideas: *I work to live, not live to work. There will be enough. The universe is benevolent.*

**Sphera Mundi VII
(The Jewel in the Lotus)**

Richard Sudden, 2000
Mixed media on panel
50.25" x 50.25"

"This piece is about regenerative power, with the life-giving sun at the center and the Buddhist mantra, *Om mani padme hum**, repeated twice in a clockwise direction, as the prayer wheel turns," says the artist. Indeed, the work is a meditation on life's many aspects: the creative and the receptive, science and intuition, the earth and the heavens, the unknown and the known.

*Behold, the jewel in the lotus, a reference to Avalokiteshvara, the Bodhisattva of Compassion.

I belong to a community. In your effort to take care of business, you may forget how interconnected you are to others, and they to you. This is a good time to think about the circles of family, friends, and community in which you are an integral link, perhaps directing a prayer to someone in one of those circles who would benefit from that gift.

Meditation

The earth sends its abundant energy to me, and I return it with gratitude.

This is a good standing or walking meditation, particularly if you can take your shoes off. Breathe in on "the earth sends its abundant energy to me." Breathe out on "and I return it with gratitude." Breathe deeply and rhythmically. Allow the soles of your feet to receive the impression of whatever is beneath them and the energy that comes with it. That energy will travel into your body through your legs. You will feel it travel through you as you breathe. Allow the rest of your body to receive earth energy in a similar way — in aromas and sounds, in the colors of objects around you. Maintain your center by directing your attention to one sense at a time until you are able to feel them all at once. You will feel calm but charged with energy. With each exhalation, cycle that energy back into the world.

24

Passion

The Lower Abdomen Chakra is known as the "sex chakra," because it includes the reproductive organs and the hormones that arouse passion. It is that and more. Passion is the sexual desire that flows through lovers. Passion is also the devotion that flows through friends and family, and the ardor that fuels dreams and ideas. This chakra is the center of strong feelings, both positive and negative: joy, grief, desire, anger, and, yes, sexual ecstasy. It is also the center of creativity, which draws on each of these passions for expression.

The Lower Abdomen Chakra

The second chakra connects from your astral body to the place on your spine between your tailbone and just below your navel.

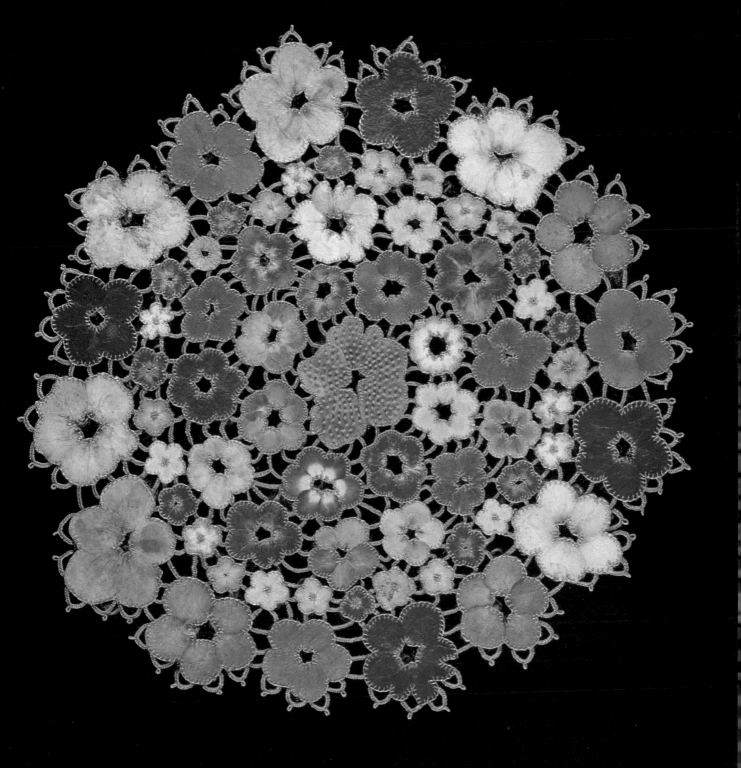

Rainbow Serpent

Susanne Iles, 2000
Acrylic on board, 20" x 15"

The second chakra is about relationships, connections. "The Australian Aboriginal people believe the universe has two aspects: the physical world, and another from which it is derived called the Dreamtime. The Dreamtime recognizes that every life process, event or activity leaves behind something of itself ," says Iles. The serpent is a bridge that connects both worlds, past to present, heaven to future.

"Sometimes I wonder: Did the painting come about because I was the Dreamer...or the Dreamed?"

Physically it is a center that energizes all the lower-torso organs, including the reproductives, spleen, kidneys, and bladder.

Emotionally passions evoke not only strong urges but the strength to express them. Creativity springs from the Lower Abdomen Chakra in the same way that new life emerges from the uterus. There is even a painting in this chapter that expresses just this idea. The lower torso is also our center of gravity, so we may think of this chakra as an emotional gyroscope. (With pornography and sexual repression at the opposite extremes of this chakra, you can see the importance of balance.)

Spiritually by way of Tantric yoga, the second chakra reminds us that passion is sacred. This chakra draws from the ones above and below it, empowering you to give and take in equal measure. And isn't that the essence of the best relationships?

Vibrations

The theme of interconnectedness continues into color itself.

Light: Orange, the color of the second chakra, is nestled in the spectrum between two primaries, red and yellow, as a combination of the two. Orange also includes pastels such as coral, and earth tones such as ocher and rust.

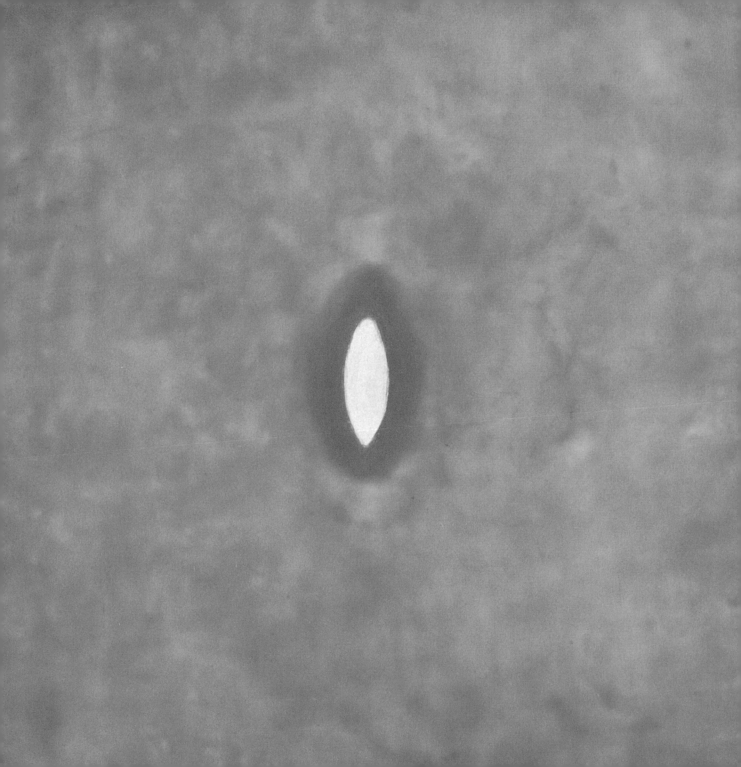

Lotus Crossing

Barbara Ellmann, 1999
Encaustic on nine wooden panels
64" x 64"

The Parcheesi gameboard has been a visual touchstone for Ellmann. After viewing an exhibition of traditional mandalas, she pondered the similarity of the two. "I wondered if Parcheesi, a child's game, contained in its simple geometry some connection to the sacred religious form. When I was introduced to Hindu *yantras*, geometric diagrams for spiritual meditation, the associations became richer, she says, noting, "The daily practice of painting is itself a meditation."

Give and Take

(previous spread)
Miriam Karp, 1999
Encaustic on panel, 28" x 48"

This painting perfectly expresses the creative energy of the second chakra. Says the artist, "*Give and Take* was the first painting I did when I went back to the studio after the birth of my daughter, Isabella. It is intended as a birth painting to celebrate the utter mystery I felt in producing the new life. The painting's colors, meant to be both vaginal and dawn-like, express creation on the most intimate scale of the body and the overall creation of the world, to which I was feeling so powerfully connected."

Sound: The vibration that resonates for this chakra is VAM (with the *a* as in *ah*) in the tone of D. If you don't know the tone scale, try O (as in *god*) in whichever key is comfortable for your voice. Inhale. Begin your intonation on the exhale. Feel the sound fill your throat and mouth as it passes into the space around you.

Matter: Orange stones, such as amber, coral, and carnelian, have a complementary vibration. You may want to meditate while holding one of these stones, or simply wear a piece of jewelry set with one of them.

Contemplations

Love is the focus for these centered thoughts.

Sex and love. We want them both, and we deserve them both, but sometimes they're not forthcoming in equal measure. We may sacrifice one for the other, and that's okay as long as we're aware that we're doing so. The colloquial idea, "Women give sex to receive love; men give love to receive sex," may not always be true, but it's worth reflecting on.

Pleasure is divine. Only puritanical thinking equates pleasure with impropriety. You have a right to feel passion, pleasure, fulfillment, con-

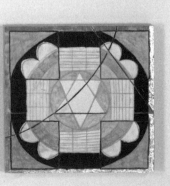

tentment. That's why the senses are fulfilled through such pleasures as food, drink, music, and dancing in rituals both sacred and mundane. Let these emotions know they're welcome in your life, and you will find them at your door.

Meditation

Creative energy is within me, yearning to be expressed.

The artworks in the book spring from energized and passionate second chakras. You have the same capacity for creativity. Select an image, perhaps from this chapter, that speaks to you and holds your gaze. Sit comfortably in front of it. Mentally scribe a circle in which you and the image are in its center. You have created a mandalic space. As you sit quietly within it, let the picture you are looking at evoke colors and images in your own mind. Close your eyes, allowing your mental images to enter your circle until it feels full. Then, mentally walking the circle clockwise, examine each of the elements that comprise your mandala. Once you have traveled through it, just bask in the energy of the mandala you have created. If you are inspired at the end of your meditation, create a tangible version of your mandala, being open to improvisation and variation.

Moclipse

Gail Gregg, 1998
Encaustic on panels, 24" x 24"

"I've been painting images of the American West as seen from 30,000 feet in the air. I'm particularly fascinated by what happens when the checkerboard lots of this landscape meet each other. Alfalfa may be planted next to soybeans or wheat. Farmers may erect fences or build roads to divide neighboring lots, or they might do nothing at all," says Gregg. In *Moclipse*, the borders create a center, a whole. "Their unity suggests that the common ground underneath is more potent than the artificial divisions above."

SELF-ESTEEM

Big Bang

Patrick Weisel, 2001
Mixed media, 10" x 10"

"*Big Bang* is a meditation on the moment just after the beginning of the universe — the moment differences begin, the moment boundaries and individuality begin, perhaps the moment the universe fell from grace," says the artist. "According to the Big Bang Theory, the entire universe came from a single point called a singularity, a point so small it had no dimension. When astronomers try to find the original position of this singularity—which is to say, the center of the universe—it turns out to be everywhere. For me, the Big Bang Theory supports the Hindu idea that differences are merely illusion. All is one."

Each chakra builds on the one before it, so the Solar Plexus Chakra is the place where instinct and passion are shaped by ego and will into a particular personality. It is the place where the person you know as you is centered. In the same way that a wet clay pot goes into the kiln and emerges a fully-formed vessel, ego and will, the motivators of the third chakra, have fired you as a vessel of feeling and intellect with a sense of self—and the capacity for self-esteem. Unlike that finished pot, however, you are a work in progress, developing that sense of self throughout your life.

The Solar Plexus Chakra

The Solar Plexus, a network of nerves, is located in the abdominal

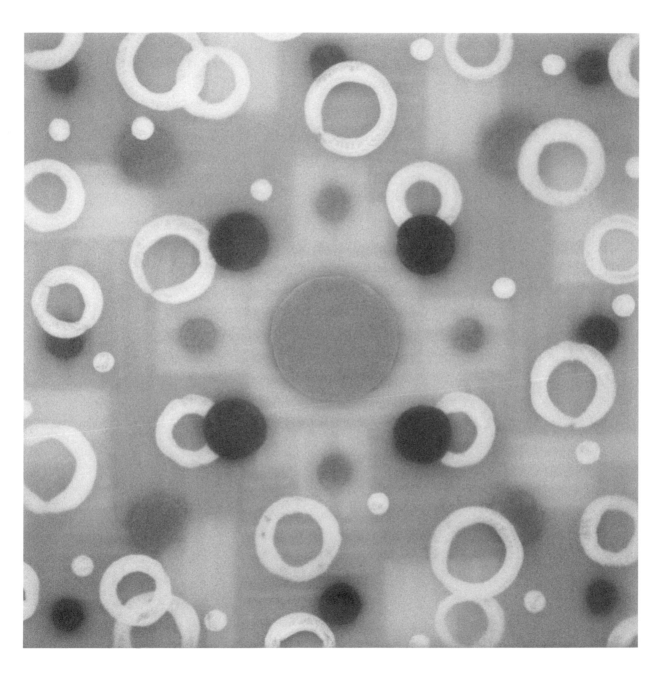

Yellow Green Ring

Linda Daniels, 2000
Monotype, 27" x 27"

"Paint embellishes and adorns; it serves to complete an object or idea," says the artist. "I hope my work provides a palpable optical experience. An experience that leads the viewer to feel the pleasure derived from looking." Pleasure is a wonderful conduit to centering, for to feel pleasure, we must be open. And in being open, we can release negative energy—tension, anger, fear—while being receptive to vibrations of a higher order.

cavity above the navel and below the heart. This is where the third chakra connects to the body.

Physically the Solar Plexus Chakra energizes the middle-torso organs: stomach, liver, gall bladder, digestive system and autonomic nervous system. The reason you can get sick to your stomach at the mere idea of something unpleasant owes to the strong neural/visceral connection here.

Emotionally this is the locus of your gut instinct, the insistent feeling in the pit of your stomach that has the power to temper, even overrule, the logic of reason. (A well-tuned gut instinct is also smart enough to face facts.) It is the place where id urges—overindulgence and unchecked emotions—are controlled by more reasoned thinking. If the second chakra provides the impetus for creative expression, the third chakra channels the power to create and achieve ever loftier goals. Power is also a third chakra issue. Are you controlling? Do you feel controlled? How do you deal with authority and responsibility? These are questions to contemplate as the artwork in this chapter helps you clear a path to your Solar Plexus Chakra.

Yellow Grain Rug   Linda Davis 2000

Spirituall**y** centered energy in this chakra enables you to experience a mind-body connection — to feel whole, to feel comfortable in your skin — and reminds you that the capacity to love yourself is the first step in being able to love others.

Vibrations

Reverberation is particularly powerful at this chakra, because the solar plexus is so close to the diaphragm, that band of muscle which expands and contracts with each breath and vibrates with sound.

Light: "Solar" is an appropriate word since the chromatic vibration of the Solar Plexus Chakra is yellow, the symbolic color of the sun. Surely it is not coincidental that "sunny" yellow is a mood elevator. Allow this hue via the artwork in this chapter to affect you similarly.

Sound: The vibration that resonates for this chakra is RAM (with the *a* as in *ah*) in the tone of E. Alternately, try O (as in *oh*) in whichever key is comfortable for you.

Matter: Yellow stones such as citrine and topaz, as well as the metal gold, have a complementary vibration to this chakra. If you are drawn to the color yellow, or to third-chakra issues, you may want to wear a

Beauty and the Beast

Gloria Klein, 1986
Acrylic on canvas, 60" x 60"

Klein's work is about bringing order to complexity in her painting and in her life. "I work with a system to distribute color and form," she says. "This system enables me to get out of the noisy world I live in, to withdraw into myself. The activity of creating colorful, strong images brings peace."

40

yellow stone in a gold setting, such as a pendant suspended low over the solar plexus, as you center yourself at this chakra.

Contemplations

Power, ego, and control are the issues for the Solar Plexus Chakra.

Am I good enough? Will I succeed? Am I a fraud? Do you like me? Even on a good day, self-doubts can bubble up from the first and second chakras, source of unarticulated fears and strong emotions, respectively. It takes the self-esteem of the third chakra to dispel those negative thoughts. As you center here, consider all the ways you are good enough.

Enough about you; let's talk about me. On the flip side, sometimes the ego is working overtime. If that's the case, take a few moments to appreciate the wonderful qualities in those closest to you. And when you're finished, ask them how their day was.

Responsibility is like champagne; it works best when shared. If you consistently take on too much responsibility, ask yourself why you need to be so in control. If you never assume any responsibility, ask yourself what you're afraid of.

Symbiosis VIII

Joanne Mattera and Patrick Weisel, 1995
Wax, enamel, pins on Plexiglas
12" x 12"

Working with yellow—the color of the Solar Plexus Chakra, which relates to issues of ego and will—two artists transcended individual egos to collaborate on a mutually expressive series of work. Mattera, who employs orderly progressions, relaxed to accommodate Weisel's meandering line. Weisel, in turn, accepted the rigors of a superimposed system. The result—"the boundary between chaos and order," Weisel calls it—expanded the aesthetic possibilities of each artist.

42

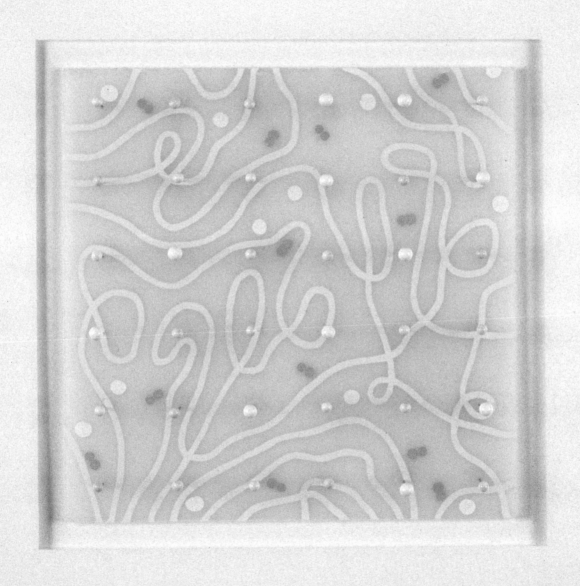

Meditation

I am Solid as a Rock but Light as Air

Select an artwork from this or another chapter to give you a focus for your energy and thoughts. As you sit, bring your hands to your Solar Plexus. (This position may be the one you unconsciously assume when you're troubled.) Do your shoulders feel heavy? No wonder, there's a boulder there. Direct your thoughts so that they act as a fulcrum to dislodge it. Gently, insistently, lever this mass until you feel it slide off and roll off the mountain that is you. Imagine it breaking up into tiny pieces as it rolls down. Don't worry, it's not going to hurt anyone. Breathe deeply. The solid mass that was pressing on your shoulders has been replaced by centering energy that is buoying you from within. You may want to reflect on that broken boulder now. Whatever it once was — too much responsibility, too little self-esteem, over-attachment to material things — is now a mass of harmless pebbles far from your mental mountaintop.

When you feel "pressed" and there's no time to sit and center, take a few moments to draw the universe into you by breathing. Imagine little pockets of air between your vertebrae, gently stretching your spine.

Labyrinth #12

Ellen Oppenheimer, 1997
Fabric quilt, 37" x 37"

Plying strong geometry and dense patterns, Oppenheimer works to achieve "a particular arrangement of line and balance of color" in her quilts. Her convoluted line eventually returns to itself. On an allegorical level, she notes that the return to a starting point is often true for life journeys as well. "Patterns," she says, "usually repeat themselves."

44

COMPASSION

The fourth chakra is governed by equilibrium and balance, starting with its symbol: Within a circle evenly surrounded by twelve petals, there are two overlapping triangles, one pointing up and the other pointing down. The upward triangle represents the bottom three chakras. The downward triangle represents the top three chakras. The triangles merge to form a six-pointed star. In the middle of the star is a hexagram representing the middle chakra—the Heart Chakra—our center of compassion. The Heart Chakra is also the center that allows us to appreciate and be moved by artistic expression.

The Heart Chakra

The fourth chakra extends from your astral body to a point on your spinal column just behind your heart.

Green Bloom

Martin Kline, 1999
Encaustic on panel
30" x 30" x 4"

Spring green is the color of the first new shoots of the season. Radiating petal forms, so like depictions of the chakras, evoke a blossoming of the spirit. "There was a hypnotic and trance-like action in the making of this painting," says the artist, who developed the work slowly from the center, brushstroke by brushstroke. "It was almost like prayer."

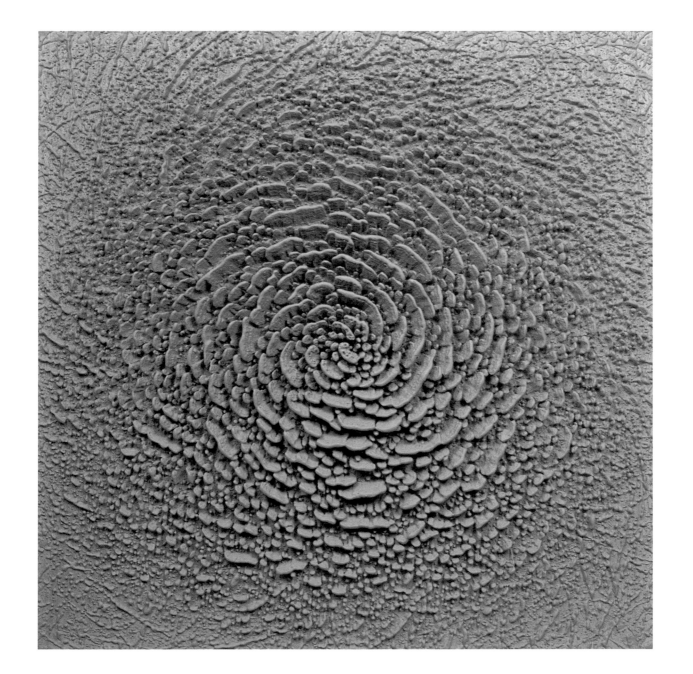

Requiem for Monarch IV

Nancy Clearwater Herman, 2000
Computer images on fabric
40" x 40"

"Although I am not a religious person, I find spiritual peace in the contemplation of symmetrical images," says Herman. She uses the form of the mandala because it represents time, and illustrates that an action that takes place at the center, radiates outward and "reverberates through time and space in unimaginable but ever-multiplying ways." This work's lively pattern created by the print of U.S. currency "concerns the genetic engineering of seeds and their subsequent threat to the environment." A contemplation of this image might include some thought about our own compassion for green and growing things.

Physically it is the energizing center for the upper torso, including the heart, lungs, and skin. If you have trouble imagining the chakras, which cycle the energy of the universe to and through you, you need only to consider the beating heart as it cycles blood through your body in essentially the same way. Blood is just more tangible than *prana*, the etheric life force of the universe. Prana, a yogic term, is also known as *ch'i* or *qi*, as in *ta'i ch'i* and *qi gong*. That's why conscious breathing, as opposed to the reflexive intake of oxygen and outflow of carbon dioxide, is so essential to centering.

Emotionally the Heart Chakra is open to unconditional love that radiates from heart and mind. And love is so strong that its effects (or lack of them) can be felt through the generations. So connected is the metaphysical chakra to our physical pump, that *kind hearted, warm hearted, whole hearted, soft hearted* (or their opposites) describe emotional states of being energized by this chakra.

Spiritually the heart is open and all-embracing. It is passion on a higher level: compassion. This chakra allows us to give, to forgive, to accept. It is the gateway to our higher selves. Ecumenically, the six-pointed star that is the symbol of the Heart Chakra is also a yantra for tantric meditation and the Jewish Star of David.

48

Vibrations

Spring, the time when new shoots emerge from the earth, is the vibrational complement to the Heart Chakra with its green color and growth-focused energy. We can look to fourth-chakra energy as we seek to develop emotionally and spiritually.

Light: Green is the color of the Heart Chakra. Green is also the color of money. Prosperity paired with generosity is energizing for both giver and receiver. So why are depictions of the heart, as in valentines, always colored red? Artists will tell you that red is the complement to green; that these colors are opposites on the color wheel. Not surprisingly, the union of opposites is a spiritual theme.

Sound: The vibration that resonates for this chakra is YAM (with the *a* as in *ah*) in the tone of F. Alternately, try A (as in *apple*) in whichever key is comfortable for you. Feel the sound deep within your chest as it resonates in harmony with the beat of your heart.

Matter: Green stones such as jade, emerald, malachite and tourmaline have a complementary vibration to this chakra. To help you center here, wear a pin or necklace over your heart, or finger a mala rosary made from a heartwood such as rosewood or sandalwood.

Jotting 21

Donna Sharrett, 2000
Monotype, 20.75" x 20.75"

Meditative in their making, symbolic in their meaning, Sharrett's mandalas embody a fullness forged of loss. "The cyclical aspects of our cultural habits, of traditions observed and ritually followed, offer a continuum with the past," she says. "The roundness symbolizes life and hope as well as the cycles that connect life and death." The heart's unlimited capacity to love ensures that those we hold dearest will remain with us for all time.

Echo

Cheryl Goldsleger, 1999
Wax, oil, pigment on paper
22" x 22"

With its motif of a central circle repeated in four corners, Echo calls to mind a minimalist version of a Tibetan mandala. "Echo is based on maze or labyrinth structures," says the artist. "In this piece, two different structures are intertwined. My interest is to create a dialog in which the shift in color, shape, and emphasis create a sense of progression and transition. The need to mentally walk through these interconnected spaces is important. One may find oneself lost or confused, back where one started, or making progress. All are viable possibilities."

Contemplations

Love is the focus for our centered thoughts.

Love is unconditional. Love is such a valuable offering that it tends to come with strings attached. As in "heartstrings." As in "I'll love you more if..." It's bribery. As we center ourselves at our Heart Chakra, it's worth examining why an emotion so abundant, so replenishing, needs to have such a heavy tax imposed on it. Tax? Bribery? How did love get to be associated with extortion anyway?

How do I love? Let me count the ways. We're bombarded with ooh-ooh-baby in music and movies, in novels and on TV, but romance is a sliver of the sentiment spectrum. Yes, romantic love is powerful, but we are also deeply satisfied by familial and platonic love, and by our feelings for particular places and activities. Each of those loves has a place in our heart so that we need never live without joy. What are the loves of your life?

Today I am grateful for. . . This simple contemplation is like saying grace, except instead of offering thanks before a meal, you can offer it any time during the smorgasbord of life that the universe has laid before you.

Quo Vadis?

Amy Cheng, 1998
Oil, oil stick, silkscreen on canvas
24" x 24"

The title in Latin means *Where are you going?* "While working on the painting, it was my intent to locate myself as a speck in the universe, akin to the Zen concept of 'nothing and everything.' I hold to a system of spiritual beliefs and I make a conscious attempt to reflect that system in my artwork," says Cheng. "My paintings simultaneously refer to nature, the cosmos, and inner states of consciousness."

Meditation

Forgiveness Makes the Heart Grow Fuller

Air is the element associated with the Heart Chakra, and prana is the vivifying element in air — so begin this meditation with conscious breathing. As you fully inhale and exhale, envision the Heart Chakra as a brilliant green bud unfolding outward just over the center of your chest. This blossom is fed by the love that flows from your heart. The more freely the love flows, the more fully the petals open. Acknowledge that apprehension or resentment may be intertwined with your love, particularly in the feelings you hold toward those you care for the most. Forgiveness is the vivifying element in love, so imagine the negative feelings as a few coarse outer leaves to be clipped from this glorious flower. Don't dwell on those coarse leaves. Focus on the blossoming flower as prana fills your being, and you will find that those outer leaves fall away on their own. As much as you can, allow this fully-blossomed flower to accompany you into everyday life and to remain open above your heart.

54

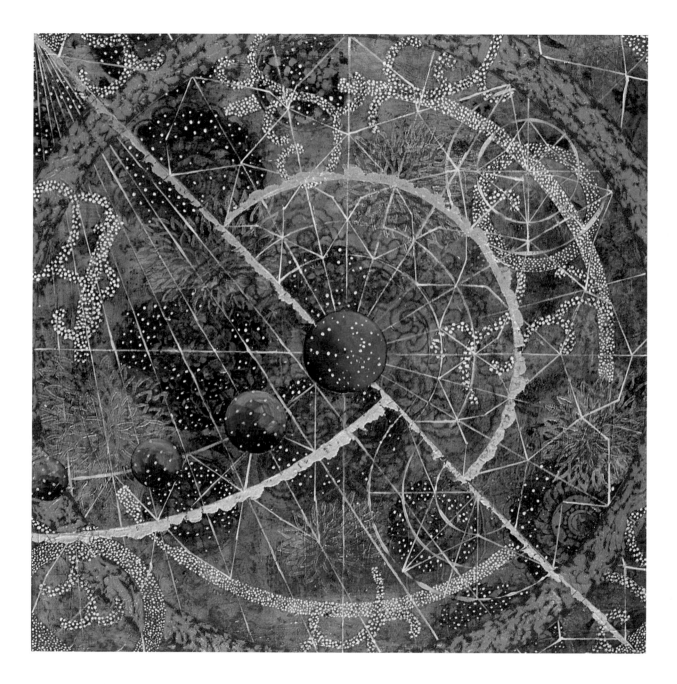

Expression

"Express Yourself" is the message of the fifth chakra. Physically, the Throat Chakra empowers you to speak up and speak out, to communicate in any medium in which you can express your feelings and ideas. This is the chakra that energizes teachers, public speakers, writers, filmmakers, and performing and visual artists. Body language and dance also come from the fifth chakra. Metaphysically, the Throat Chakra empowers you to communicate in another way: to listen. As you look at the artwork on these pages, for instance, you may want to spend time with each one to "hear" visually what it has to say to you. And should you be moved to respond, you have many vocabularies with which to respond—from sound, words, and movement, to creating an image of your own.

Deco Pinwheel II

Patsy Allen, 1986
Fabric quilt, 76" x 77"

"Much of my work has a central focus, very often an X that divides the quilt into four sections, as here. I had been using this motif for some time before I discovered it was called a 'tumbling cross.' For years I refused to acknowledge that these crosses were anything but design elements," says the artist. Still, their recurrence intrigued her, and sitting quietly with a commissioned quilt is the last step before she packs it up and ships it off.

56

Herd Map 3

Madeline Metz, 2001
Acrylic on canvas, 90" x 90"

"Nature and spirituality are one
and the same. Signals and les-
sons are available for those who
can still themselves long enough
to perceive them," says the artist,
who has drawn inspiration from
animals for her painting. "I was
painting mandalas years before I
had knowledge of what they are.
Although others can use my paintings for meditation, I cannot. The
process of painting such a large
work stroke by stroke is a
meditation in itself."

The Throat Chakra

The fifth chakra extends from your astral body to a place on your spine just behind the throat.

Physically its energy includes the shoulders, neck, jaw, larynx, bronchial system, and thyroid. A deep sigh or moan is this chakra's way of letting you express yourself when you don't have the words, perhaps when you don't even realize you have something to say.

Emotionally the fifth chakra encourages you to give voice to your feelings — to laugh and cry freely, to express surprise or displeasure — and to perceive and respond to those feelings in others. It is here that you seek to understand.

Spiritually the Throat Chakra is the gateway to a higher state of being where sound gives way to silence. Like the heart below and the Third Eye above, it is an intuitive center that does not require words for communication. It is a place from which to pray aloud or silently.

Vibrations

The vibration of this chakra is sound. Speech and song are generated from the throat, and you will find chanting or humming to be profoundly

complementary to your centering here. You may also be moved by the spiritual sounds of others, such as American gospel singing, Buddhist chants, Santeria invocations and rhythms, or Arabic *qawalli* music. It's not coincidental that song and ritual are closely intertwined in spiritual and secular ceremonies, and that many such celebrations take place within the space of a circle.

Light: The color for the Throat Chakra is blue — celestial, cyan, turquoise, electric, royal — all the colors you see in the artworks of this chapter. Allow yourself to experience these hues, for they are as vast as the heavens and as deep as the sea.

Sound: The vibration that resonates most strongly for this chakra is HAM (with the *a* as in *ah*) in the tone of G. Alternately, try EH (as in *ebb*) in whichever key is comfortable for you.

Matter: Blue stones such as aquamarine and turquoise have a complementary vibration to this chakra. To help you center here, you might wear a blue stone at your neck, or maybe a brilliant blue scarf. And since the hands are a medium of expression, consider a blue-stone ring or bracelet.

Harmony Hammond, 1997
Oil, fabric on canvas, 56" x 52"

Painter, sculptor, teacher, activist, lesbian, feminist, mother, grandmother, t'ai ch'i adept, writer, and more, Hammond has brought all of these identities to her work. Without ascribing a meaning to this painting that was not intended by the artist herself, we may nonetheless meditate on the image in fifth chakra terms. The ring of brilliant blue suggests this center's energy—communication, inspiration, speaking truth—while its enclosure of red and yellow suggest that empowered Throat Chakra expression comes from a physical self that is grounded (first chakra) and an ego that is centered (third chakra).

Contemplations

Talking and listening are the themes for these centering contemplations:

What do you want to tell yourself? Not "drop off the dry-cleaning" or who made you angry today, but what's really on your mind. Normally the soundtrack for your concerns is a stream-of-consciousness ramble of complaints and comments. You'll need to do some mental sorting — to listen and then talk to yourself with composure, as if you are talking to a friend — which, of course, you are.

Is there someone with whom you haven't been communicating well? Think about what you would like to hear this person say to you, then dig a little deeper to intuit what she or he would actually say. But why wonder? It may be time for a face-to-face (and heart-to-heart) conversation.

Be heard. When you are centered at the Throat Chakra, you are empowered to express yourself in ways you may have only imagined. Having developed strength at each of the lower chakras, you'll realize you not only have a right to expression but very likely something to say. Your contemplation is simply, *What do I want to say, and how do I want to say it?*

62

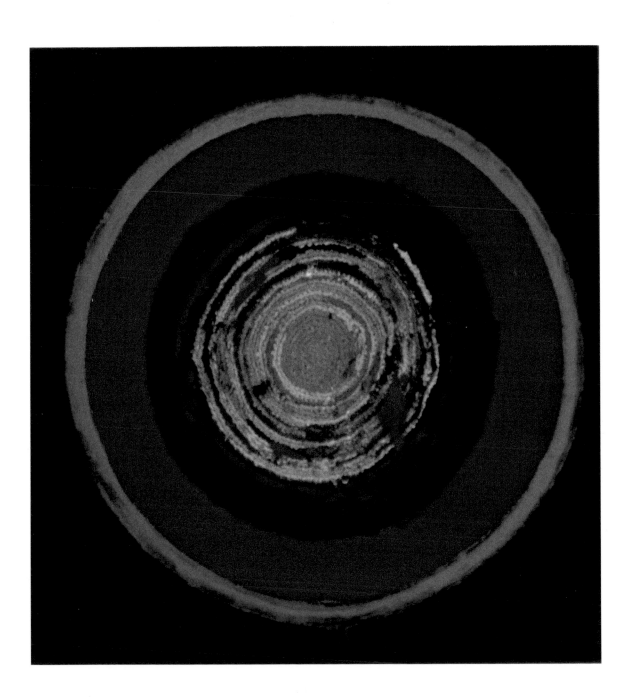

Occhio Blu

Joanne Mattera, 2001
Encaustic on panel, 12" x 12"

"Much of my painting consists of two elements: a simple image and a complex, multilayered surface. The result is a sensuous minimalism in which the opposites amplify one another," says Mattera. "While there is no intended spiritual message in my work, its contrary elements reflect my own personal yin/yang: a spirit-focused core around which swirls an overscheduled, multidirectional life." This image is a reminder to stop and center as well as a visual means to get there.

Meditation

I Am Wrapped in a Blanket of Noiseless Sound

This meditation is simply to listen. Its beauty is that you can do it anywhere. For instance, sit in a quiet, low-lit room, perhaps with one of the images from this book to help you gather your energy to yourself. You may want to turn off your telephones. Let the sound around you — the hum of the refrigerator, a car passing on the street — filter through you without disturbing you. Breathe rhythmically and deeply, feeling your upper torso expand and contract, aware that the air you take in is full of prana, the energy of the universe. Just sit and breathe, inhaling and exhaling. The white noise will disappear and you'll be wrapped in a soft blanket of noiseless sound. There's no time limit. Sit quietly in this way until your body brings you back to the present. If at that point you are moved to commune verbally with the universe, try chanting EH or HAM, the sounds that most strongly resonate for the Throat Chakra.

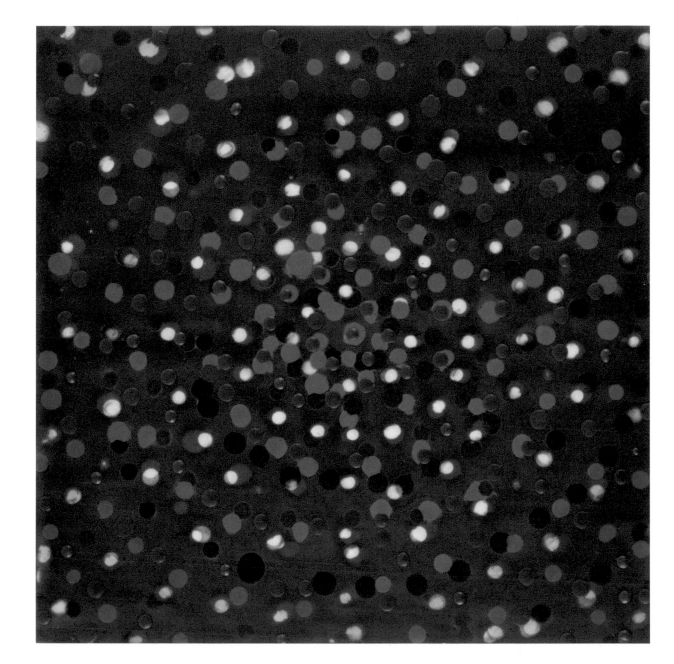

PERCEPTION

"I see," you say when you understand. Perception beyond the tangible—whether as insight, visionary thinking, dreams, intuition, or clairvoyance—is centered in the sixth chakra, also known as the Third Eye Chakra. This is where the energies of a higher order interact with everyday self. The Third Eye is not just a spiritual portal for psychics and swamis, but for anyone who has a sense of something greater and a longing to be a part of it.

The Third Eye Chakra

The sixth chakra extends from your astral body to your physical body behind the brow, just between the eyes. The pineal gland is located in the same spot, and although its exact function is not known, a neural connection exists between it and the eyes via the optic nerve.

Hungry Eye

Benjamin Long, 1995
Oil, mixed media, 43" x 43"

"Religion has always been a part of my life. I'm the son of a clergyman. Most of the time I'm not trying to make this part of my life obvious in my work but it's in the background, as is the thought that my abilities are a gift," says Long.

"Hungry Eye is about looking at the way an artist looks: obsessively, taking in as much as possible." Fittingly for the sixth chakra, site of the Third Eye, this painting is also about looking inward. "It can be read as emanating from and/or zeroing in on a centered, spiritual self that can't be seen visually."

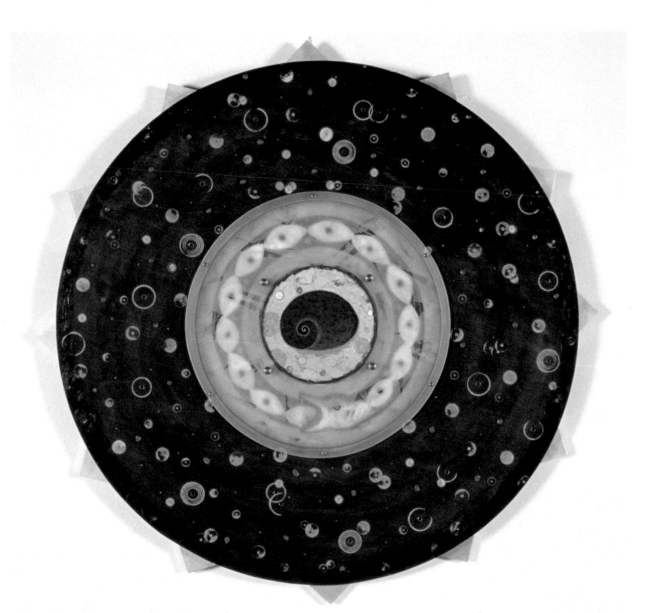

Physically Third Eye energy encompasses not only the eyes but the face and the anatomy behind it, such as sinuses, olfactory glands, the pituitary gland, and the brain itself.

Emotionally the sixth chakra is the receptor for our sixth sense, where psychic energy channels into the physical body. While intuition is felt in the Throat and Heart chakras, and even in the Solar Plexus as a gut response, this is the locus of true telepathy.

Spiritually the sixth chakra is the center in which our longing for the ethereal is recognized. It is the portal through which we must pass whether we are going back to our religious roots or forward onto a new spiritual path.

Vibration

The frequency of light is the vibration that resonates for the Third Eye. Meditating on a visual image is called *yantra yoga*, and while serious practitioners require specific kinds of geometric images, you will find all the images in this book to be conducive to centering this chakra. Look at the artwork in this book with your Third Eye — that is, in an intuitive or clairvoyant way — and you may see something quite different from what your two eyes show you.

Wave

Henry Leo Schoebel, 2000
Urethane on canvas, 20" x 20"

"Physicists have postulated that the beginning of Creation was caused by a break in the symmetry of Nothing. In physics, Nothing, it seems, is the most symmetrical thing in the universe. It is this perfection that renders Nothing beyond human perception," says Schoebel. "Accordingly, Nothing becomes Something only when its symmetry is broken—perhaps Creation! I employ the shape of the circle in my paintings as a metaphor for the invisible Nothing within which Creation lies hidden."

Serpentine

(previous spread)
Joanne Mattera, 2001
Encaustic on panel, 12" x 24"

"When working on this painting I had the peculiar and wonderful sensation of being out of my body," says the artist. "As I was brushing on layers of pigmented wax and then scraping some off to reveal the spiral, I had the distinct feeling of floating over the polar icecap. Later, working on the blue side, I felt myself being pulled into its depth." You may want to explore the strong push/pull of this painting for yourself. Select a panel, sit quietly, and follow its path until your mental chatter subsides; then allow yourself to be gently transported to a quieter realm.

Light: Indigo, a dark blue that tends toward purple, is the color of the Third Eye Chakra. It is slightly mysterious, like Third Eye vision.

Sound: The vibration that resonates most strongly for this chakra is KSHAM in the tone of A (the *k* is not pronounced but serves as a throat stop before uttering *sham*, with the *a* as in *ah*). Alternately, try EE (as in *beet*) in whichever key is comfortable for you. Let the sound resonate through the roof of your mouth and into the space behind your forehead.

Matter: Dark blue stones such as lapis lazuli, sodalite and sapphire have a complementary vibration.

Contemplations

What are your dreams telling you? Dreams are messengers of what we already know but haven't yet realized. The brief period between waking and sleep is a good time for intuiting your dreams, because you are receptive to their messages. Is there an image that visits you regularly, or one so powerful that it stays with you? Look at it with your Third Eye.

What do you long for? Where the desires of the second chakra are physical and emotional, those of the sixth chakra have a more spiritual frequency. What beckons you? Can you visualize the road to it?

Diamond in the Box

Nancy Clearwater Herman, 1999
Fabric quilt, 48" x 48"

Herman's work began with a desire to "paint music." She devised a formula for equating time with space and each note with a specific color. "I began in the middle and painted from there out to the edge, each note touched only by the one before it and the one after it. I began to use fabric, because I felt that specific fabric could best represent notes and instruments—that is, velvet is rich in dark tones, and satin in light ones," she says. "In this work, two progressions of color and pattern move through each other. They maintain a tension of separate entities while harmonizing into one visual statement."

Meditation

Seeing with the Third Eye

Spiritual vision springs from an energized Third Eye Chakra. Try this twilight meditation in a quiet spot where you'll feel comfortable letting night fall around you. Begin by centering your gaze on an image from this chapter. Inhale and exhale, taking in the energy of the universe. As your meditation space darkens, turn your gaze within. Your Third Eye will open to a purifying white light. It will illuminate the space behind your brow and shine on the Throat, Heart, and Solar Plexus Chakras. The light is cool, and as it mixes with the prana from every breath, you'll realize that the light and the prana are one and the same. Let this energy travel to your Lower Abdomen and Root Chakras so that your entire physical body is illuminated from within. Breathe freely in and out, remaining in this state for as long as your Third Eye visualizes the light. When the light has dimmed, open your physical eyes slowly. Sit quietly in the darkness until you feel reintegrated into your physical surroundings.

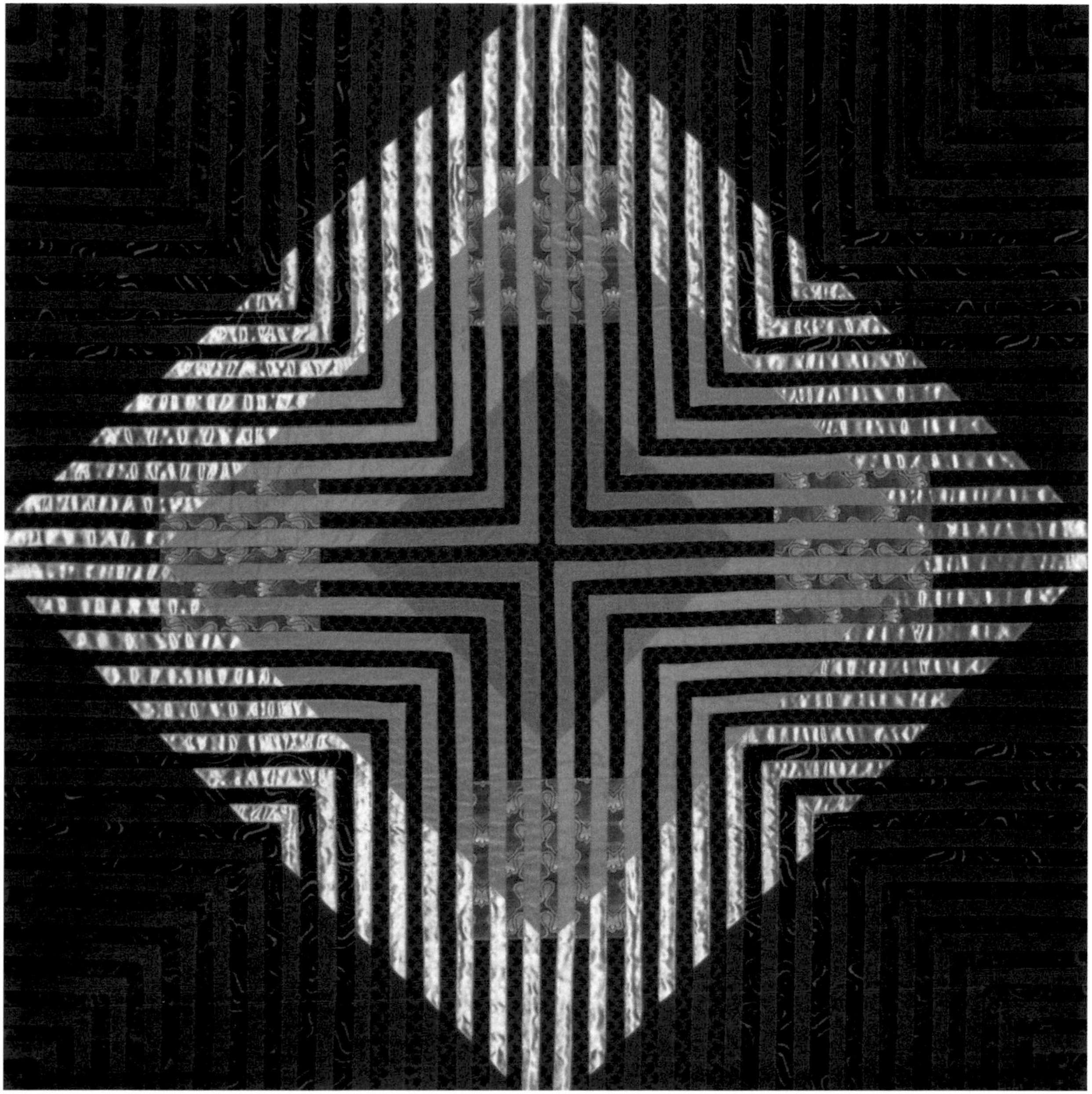

SPIRITUALITY

Described by Hindu and Buddhist mystics as the thousand-petaled lotus, the Seventh Chakra opens upward on your astral body just above the crown of your head. It is the sacred spot where you end and the universe begins. Humans seem to know this intuitively. Seekers on many different paths over the ages have regarded the crown as special, marking the spot with hairdos and headdresses that extend the head a few inches closer to heaven. In the iconographies of many religions, the halo signifies holiness. The connection between chakra, headdress, and halo reminds us that the light of divinity, however sought or expressed, is clear and true.

The Crown Chakra

An open Crown Chakra is the culmination of the energy of all

the other chakras. It may take a lifetime (or many) to achieve transcendence, but in opening yourself to it, you make it possible.

Physically the Crown Chakra is the meta-brain, the ethereal extension of the physical you. You have a halo here yourself. You may not be able to see it (yet), but spiritually gifted individuals have seen and described it.

Emotionally the seventh chakra represents wisdom beyond knowledge, love beyond even compassion, existence beyond physical life.

Spiritually the Crown Chakra is the portal through which you transcend the physical world. You may experience many transcendent moments in a lifetime — feel touched, in other words, by the divine.

Vibrations

Just as indigo moves into purple in the sixth chakra, violet moves into white here in the seventh. The mutability of these colors is a lovely reminder that nothing is fixed. Vibrations by their very nature exist as movement.

Light: White light is the total of all the visible light rays. You know this if you use a prism to separate sunlight into its spectral components.

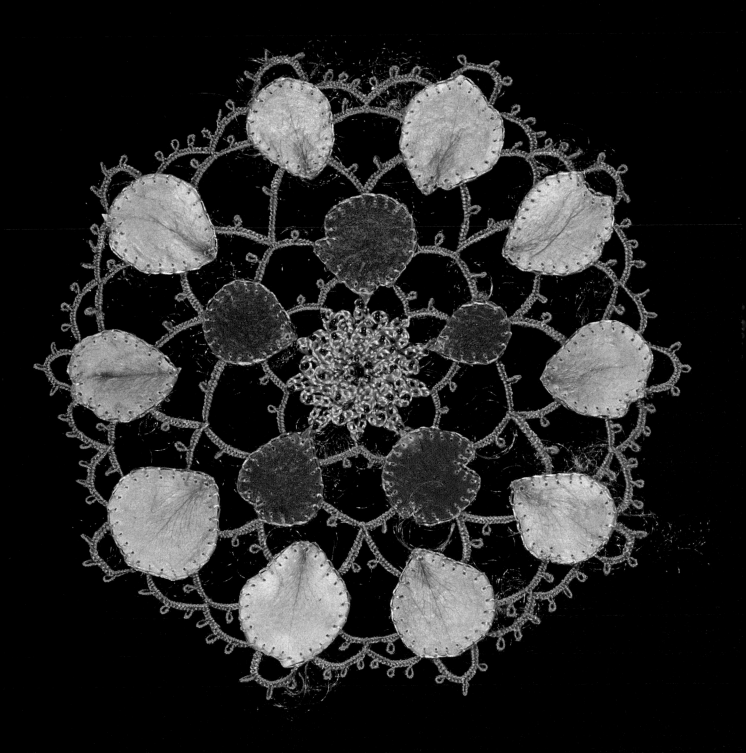

The colors of the artworks in this chapter are thus violet and the sum total of all visible colors, white.

Sound: Just as white is essence of all colors, AUM (or OM) is the essence of all sounds. This is the primordial intonation — as in, "In the beginning was the word" — and it resonates most fully at the Crown Chakra. Chant AUM in any tone that resonates for you. Inhale. As you exhale, begin with *ah* emanating from an open mouth. Gradually purse your lips so that the sound changes to *oo* and then bring your lips together so that *mmmm* resonates into your head and out through the crown.

Matter: Materiality is irrelevant at the spiritual level, but for those of us who have not yet attained a permanently transcendent state, amethyst or clear quartz crystals have a complementary vibration to the Crown Chakra. You may also wish to hold a faceted prism that can be used to refract the light.

Contemplations
Extending beyond the boundary of your skin is the theme of these contemplations.

Sunkist

Lane Twitchell, 1998
Cut paper, acrylic, mica, orange pigment, Plexiglas, 32" x 32"

The narrative meaning of this cut-paper work may be known only to the artist, but its visual layers open a window into free-associative viewing: the luminosity of a rose window, the directional clarity of a compass, the spin of a roulette wheel, the devotional detail of a Buddhist mandala.

80

Untitled

Adam Fuss, 1990
Unique Cibachrome photogram
20" x 24"

"An echo is a good way to describe the photogram, which is a visual echo of a real object," says the artist. In this untitled work, the unidentified object is subsumed by the power of its vibration: a mandala of light. Violet light is the visual expression of seventh chakra radiance. Its complementary sonic vibration is the mantra Aum, the sound of the universe; the chant of Aum begins deep within the diaphragm and radiates into infinity.

The divinity dwells within me. You are infinite. This is the meaning of the Sanskrit salutation, *Namaste*: "I honor the place in you within which the entire universe dwells." Keep this word with you to use as a reminder or greeting to yourself. You may also use it as a mantra — *nah-mas'-tay* — as you contemplate one of the images in this chapter or within the book.

I accept the scheme of the infinite. Somewhere on your to-do list or in your Power Planner make a note that the universe has a power plan of its own and you fit into it — somewhere between luck, chance, purpose, and pattern. It's called, "Go with the flow, but hang onto the oar."

Meditation

The universe sends its abundant energy to me and I return it with gratitude.

In your meditation for the Root Chakra, you received the energy of the planet through the soles of your feet. In this meditation, you will do the reverse. Take a few moments to relax into the vibrations of the Crown Chakra via image or sound. Assume a comfortable sitting posture. Close your eyes. Settle into the posture with the rhythm of your breath, being aware of each inhalation and exhalation. Now visualize

Winter Bloom

Martin Kline, 2000
Encaustic on panel, 40" x 40" x 5"

White is the color of clarity—the color of all colors, the halo that lies just above the Crown Chakra. The vertiginous swirl of petal forms, a signature for this artist, calls to mind the thousand-petaled lotus, a Buddhist symbol of enlightenment. It is difficult to separate intellectually conceived artwork from contemplative image in this luminous painting, and perhaps there's no need to try.

your crown chakra opening and the energy of the universe pouring in, filling you up, touching each chakra, and passing through your pores, as a breeze wafts through a gossamer cloth. You may imagine this energy as a stream of clear white or violet light, or perhaps as an invisible current that catches the light as a sparkling ethereal stream. This energy will flow through you as long as you choose to receive it, but there's no need to take it all at once. There is an endless supply, and you can go back whenever you want. When you are ready to complete the meditation, visualize the energy pouring over your outer body and then gradually diminishing until it is gone. Until the next time. *Namaste.*

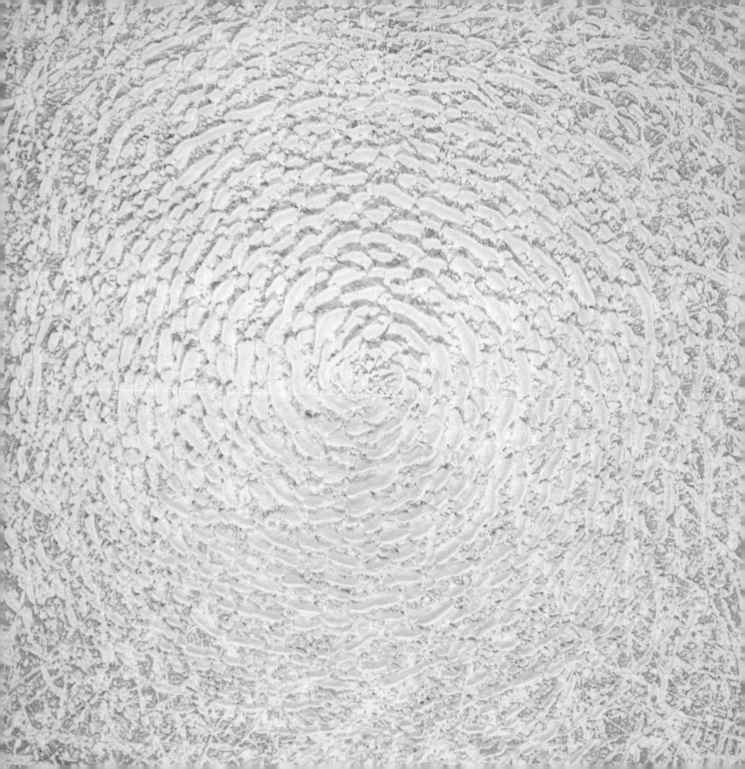

GLOSSARY

Astral Body
The mantle of energy that surrounds you, connecting your physical body to the more ethereal vibration of the universe. It is here that the chakras dwell. Also called Aura.

Aum
Aum (also Om and Amen) is the primordial sound and the essence of all sounds. It resonates most fully at the Crown Chakra, helping you to align your own vibration with the infinite.

Breath
You will find that breathing rhythmically, slowly, and fully helps your body to relax and your mind clear itself of chatter. With each breath you take in *prana*, the etheric energy of the universe.

Centering
The process by which we calm mind and body so that we are in tune with our core energy and receptive to energies of a higher order. There is no great secret to centering. You have to step off the tread mill, slow down and breathe. Contemplating a centered and symmetrical image, a *mandala* or *yantra*, will help you to find your own centered and symmetrical self.

Chakra
Chakra means *wheel* in Sanskrit. A chakra is a vortex, a wheel of energy, that extends from your etheric body to the physical body. There are seven main chakras, each with a particular color and vibration, situated along the vertical axis of the torso: the Root Chakra at the base of the spine; the Lower Abdomen Chakra at the reproductive organs; the Solar Plexus Chakra just below the sternum; the Heart Chakra in the center of the chest at heart level; the Throat Chakra behind the throat; the Third Eye Chakra behind the forehead between the eyes; and the Crown Chakra at the very top of the head. Centering yourself at each of these "stations" helps you to reach and understand the physical, emotional, and spiritual aspects of yourself there.

Chant
The vibrating repetition of a sound (mantra) or groups of sounds meant to clear the mind and to open the chakras.

Cloister
The sheltered arcade surrounding a square courtyard within the quiet confines of an abbey or church. The geometric symmetry of the cloister is a type of mandala where monastics may retreat to walk or sit in contemplation.

Contemplation
Purposeful introspection. Contemplation is more active than meditation but with a similar intent: to center the thoughts and clear the mind of all distractions.

Cross
One of the simplest mandalas: a vertical and a horizontal line that intersect at right angles. See *Religious Icons*.

Cupola
The round dome seen on many structures, notably in mosques and other places of worship, suggestive of the infinite. Stand directly under a cupola and look up; you will perceive it as a mandala.

Grounding
The physical version of centering, whereby with "feet on the ground" you draw up the energy of the earth into your body. Blood is composed largely of iron, as is the earth's core, so the connection between earth and body is primal. Grounding is a centering technique for the first chakra, the Root Chakra.

Kundalini
The life energy of the body, often represented by a snake, that lies at the base of the spine. With meditation, the kundalini rises up the spine, through the chakras, and merges with the energy from without—a union of matter and spirit—in other words, enlightenment.

Labyrinth
A circular or square pattern with a winding but unobstructed path to the center (as opposed to a *maze,* which may be constructed with baffles and dead ends). Walking a labyrinth is usually done in a spirit of contemplation. As it requires you to journey to the center and back out again, it is a means of centering yourself. The labyrinth is also a symbolic pilgrimage of life's path. There are celebrated labyrinths at the great cathedral in Chartres, France, and at Grace Cathedral in San Francisco.

Lotus
The seven chakras are depicted as lotuses with varying numbers of petals—fewer at the lower chakras, and more as they progress up the body. In Buddhism, the white lotus is a symbol for spiritual perfection. The seventh chakra, or Crown Chakra, is known as the thousand-petaled lotus. See *Chakras.*

Mandala

A symmetrical circular design used in meditation. *Mandala* means *sacred circle*. It is a symbol of infinity made comprehensible to our finite minds. Hindu and Buddhist mandalas are constructed with specific imagery to guide worshippers to specific stages of consciousness. In this book, mandalas are artworks in their own right, though they may be used for centering and contemplation.

Mantra

A one- or two-syllable sound used in meditation. Particular mantras resonate at frequencies that correspond to the vibration of particular chakras, such as *Aum* in relation to the Crown Chakra.

Medicine Wheel

Native American mandalas, constructed on the earth of stones, sticks, feathers, animal fetishes, and other objects that resonate for their makers, are meant to be compasses for body and soul.

Meditation

While there are many systems of meditation, and many visual objects—*mandalas, yantras, tankas*—aid you in meditation, you can begin by sitting quietly. In simple terms, if prayer is seen as talking to the Spirit, meditation is perceived as listening to what It has to say.

Prana

Prana (a cosmic ocean of life force) is the etheric energy that pervades and vivifies the entire universe. When we inhale and exhale, we are in communion with the universe itself.

Prayer Wheel

A hand-held Tibetan Buddhist praying instrument that consists of a metal cylinder that turns on a stick. Written on the cylinder in raised script is the mantra *Om mane padme hum*. This mantra, translated as *Hail, the Jewel in the Lotus,* is an invocation to Avalokiteshvara, the Bodhisattva of Compassion. (A boddhisattva is a being who has attained Buddhahood but who remains in human form to help others attain spiritual enlightenment.)

Religious Icons

Virtually every religion has a mandala somewhere in its folds. Not all are circles, but all direct you to their centers. Centering icons include the Christian and Celtic crosses; the Hebrew Star of David; and the Taoist *t'ai ch'i.*

Rose Window

The round stained-glass window of a Gothic cathedral, such as the one at Notre Dame or Chartres. In the dark interior of these spaces, the brilliant light radiating through the glass is a metaphor for the illumination of the soul.

Star of David

The six-pointed star, symbol of Judiasm, formed by the meshing of two triangles, one facing upward, the other facing down. Also called the *Mogen David.*

T'ai Ch'i

The Taoist symbol for the union of opposites—which is to say, the totality of all that is—a circle created by two interlocking "commas" that appear to swirl endlessly.

Tanka

Also called *thanka,* a ritual mandala painted on a cloth or fabric scroll to help Tibetan Buddhists with specific meditations.

Tantra

In Hinduism and Buddhism, the tantras are religious texts and rituals that provide worshippers with a system for spiritual practice. One of the goals of tantric practice is to raise the power of the *kundalini,* the life force, up through the chakras until it reaches the Crown Chakra in a union of matter and spirit.

Third Eye

The sixth chakra, also known as the Third Eye Chakra, extends from your astral body to your physical body behind the forehead, just between the eyes. It is associated with a visualization of the metaphysical: dreams, visions, intuition, memory, and clairvoyance.

Wheel of Fortune

The roulette of serendipity, ruled by chance or Lady Luck. It is a secularized version of the Dharma Wheel, which symbolizes the endless rounds of birth, death, and rebirth.

Yantra

A geometric figure that provides a focus for meditation. Meditating on a visual image is called *yantra yoga,* and while serious practitioners require specific kinds of images, mandalas in general help you focus and quiet your thoughts.

Yin/Yang

The Taoist concept of the union of opposites—black and white, up and down, male and female—represented by the *t'ai ch'i* symbol.

Photo Credits

Page ii: **Helix Nebula NGC 7293** by David Malin. Courtesy of the photographer and Anglo-Australian Observatory, New South Wales.

Page vi: **Snowbows** by Tom Dietrich/Aperture Geographics. Courtesy of the photographer.

Page viii and small front cover image: **Vortex** by Nelda Warkentin. Photo by John Tuckey. Courtesy of the artist.

Page 2: **Sunflower** by Camilla Smith. Courtesy of the photographer and Rainbow. Collection of Rainbow.

Page 2: **Pine Cone;** Page 3: **Snowflake;** Page 5: **Nautilus Shell;** Page 7: **Spiderweb** by Scott Camazine. Courtesy of the photographer.

Page 3: **DNA Helix Seen from Above** by Rainbow/UCSF. Courtesy of Rainbow.

Page 4: **Shell in Blue** by David Headley. Courtesy of the artist.

Page 6: **Symbiosis V** by Joanne Mattera and Patrick Weisel. Photo by Adam Reich. Courtesy of the artists.

Page 8: **Raindrops on a Pond** by Charlene Marsh. Photo by the artist. Collection of Indiana Orthopedics and Sports Medicine. Courtesy of the artist.

Page 9: **Brain Cells Firing** by Hank Morgan/Rainbow. Courtesy of Rainbow.

Page 10: **Untitled (Sun)** by Jim Baron/The Image Finders ©. Courtesy of the photographer.

Page 11: **Spiral Nebula AAT-008** by David Malin. Courtesy of the photographer and Anglo-Australian Observatory, New South Wales.

Page 12: **The Kundalini Lotus** by Charmion von Weigand (1896-1983). Photo by Josh Nefsky. Courtesy of Michael Rosenfeld Gallery, New York City.

Page 15: **The Chakras** photograph © Photodisc, Inc.

Page 17: **Mythic America or How the West Was One** by Lane Twitchell. Collection of Susan and Michael Hort; courtesy of the artist and Lawrence Rubin, Greenberg Van Doren Fine Art, New York City.

Page 19: **The Hunter** by Nancy Azara. Photo by Merle Hoffman. Courtesy of the artist.

Page 20-21: **The Four Directions: Spirit Center** by Kay WalkingStick. Photo by Cascadilla Photo, Ithaca, New York. Courtesy of June Kelly Gallery, New York City.

Page 23: **Construction #29** by Nancy Crow. Photo by J. Kevin Fitzsimmons. Courtesy of the artist.

Page 25: **Sphera Mundi VII (The Jewel in the Lotus)** by Richard Sudden. Photo by Bart Kasten. Courtesy of Marcia Wood Gallery, Atlanta.

Page 27: **Going Home at Last: The 18th Memento** by Donna Sharrett. Courtesy of Cheryl Pelavin Fine Art, New York City.

Page 29: **Rainbow Serpent** by Susanne Iles. Photo by David Leadbitter Photography and Communications. Courtesy of the artist.

Page 30-31: **Give and Take** by Miriam Karp. Courtesy of Marcia Wood Gallery, Atlanta.

Page 33: **Lotus Crossing** by Barbara Ellmann. Photo by Peter Chin. Courtesy of the artist.

Page 35: **Moclipse** by Gail Gregg. Collection of Dow Jones Co. Courtesy of the artist.

Page 37: **Big Bang** by Patrick Weisel. Courtesy of the artist.

Page 39: **Yellow Green Ring** by Linda Daniels. Courtesy of Cheryl Pelavin Fine Art, New York City.

Page 41: **Beauty and the Beast** by Gloria Klein. Photo by Robert Puglisi. Courtesy of the artist.

Page 43: **Symbiosis VIII** by Joanne Mattera and Patrick Weisel. Photo by Adam Reich. Courtesy of the artists.

Page 45: **Labyrinth #12** by Ellen Oppenheimer. Photo by Jan Watten. Courtesy of the artist.

Page 47: **Green Bloom** by Martin Kline. Private collection, New York. Courtesy of the artist.

Page 49: **Requiem for Monarch IV** by Nancy Clearwater Herman. Courtesy of the artist.

Page 51: **Jotting 21** by Donna Sharrett. Courtesy of Cheryl Pelavin Fine Art, New York City.

Page 53: **Echo** by Cheryl Goldsleger. Courtesy of Rosenberg & Kaufman Fine Art, New York City.

Page 55 and back cover image: **Quo Vadis?** by Amy Cheng. Photo by the artist. Collection of Eva Rogers. Courtesy of the artist.

Page 57: **Deco Pinwheel II** by Patsy Allen. Photo by Steve Budman. Collection of Southern Guaranty Insurance, Montgomery, Alabama. Courtesy of the artist.

Page 59: **Herd Map 3** by Madeline Metz. Courtesy of the artist.

Page 61: **Diamond Sun/Birth of Worlds** by Marjorie Kaye. Photo by and courtesy of the artist.

Page 63: **Target I** by Harmony Hammond. Photo by Herbert Lotz. Courtesy of the artist.

Page 65 and large front cover image: **Occhio Blu** by Joanne Mattera. Photo by Robert Puglisi. Courtesy of Marcia Wood Gallery, Atlanta.

Page 67: **Hungry Eye** by Benjamin Long. Courtesy of the artist.

Page 69: **Mother of All Starfish** by Chris Kelly. Photo by Rick Anthony. Courtesy of the artist.

Page 70-71: **Serpentine** by Joanne Mattera. Photo by Ernest Oliveri. Courtesy of Marcia Wood Gallery, Atlanta.

Page 73: **Wave** by Henry Leo Schoebel. Courtesy of Chiaroscuro Gallery, Santa Fe.

Page 75: **Diamond in the Box** by Nancy Clearwater Herman. Photo by Joseph Painter. Courtesy of the artist.

Page 77: **Purple Dance Kaleidoscope** by Priscilla Bianchi. Photo by Rolando Bianchi. Courtesy of the artist.

Page 79 **There Was Your Valentine: The 44th Memento** by Donna Sharrett. Courtesy of Cheryl Pelavin Fine Art, New York City.

Page 81: **Sunkist** by Lane Twitchell. Collection of Lauren and Mark Dean Vega. Courtesy of the artist and Lawrence Rubin, Greenberg Van Doren Fine Art, New York City.

Page 83: **Untitled** by Adam Fuss. Courtesy of Cheim & Read Gallery, New York City.

Page 85: **Winter Bloom** by Martin Kline. Private collection, Athens, Greece. Courtesy of the artist.